A P E R T U R E

NUMBER 77

CONTENTS

Aperture, Inc., publishes *Aperture* at Millerton, New York 12546. Officers include President, Arthur M. Bullowa; Vice-President/Treasurer, Michael E. Hoffman; Vice-President, Production, Stevan A. Baron; Secretary, Lois Myller. Directors include the President, Vice-President/Treasurer, Shirley C. Burden, and Robert A. Hauslohner. Minor White; Editor 1952–1975.

Regular subscriptions are $17.50 for four issues in the United States and $18.50 in U.S. currency in Canada and foreign countries. Retaining subscriptions are $50.00. Sustaining subscriptions are $100.00 or more. Of these amounts, $17.50 covers the cost of the four issues; the remainder is in the nature of a gift to support an ideal in photography. Such gifts are tax-deductible. The names of Retaining and Sustaining subscribers are published for the duration of their sponsorship. Single copies may be purchased at $4.95.

People & Ideas

COLOR

In late May, a controversial exhibition of some seventy-five color photographs by William Eggleston opened at The Museum of Modern Art in New York City. Because of a booming photography market and the newspaper and magazine space being given to photography, the show was a cultural event. But a cultural event of what sort, it was difficult to tell. Word of mouth had it that "color" had arrived. Another view was that the exhibition with its Instamatic poses and fashionably banal subjects—labeled with place-names such as "Tallahatchie County, Mississippi," and "Memphis"—signaled the end of photography.

Perhaps anticipating the furor they had helped to create, the public information office of The Museum of Modern Art press release quoted from the foreword to the Eggleston catalogue by John Szarkowski, Director of the Department of Photography. Said Szarkowski: "these photographers [the new generation of photographers using color] work not as if color were a separate problem to be resolved in isolation, but rather as though the world itself existed in color, as though the blue and the sky *were* one thing."

What was Szarkowski's reaction to the unprecedented range and quantity of the responses produced by his Eggleston exhibition? "I think the important thing is that Bill is one hell of a good photographer—not that the Museum has taken a stand on color photography. We don't have a stand on color photography any more than we have a stand on 35 mm photography.

"Besides, this isn't our only color show. We had a big Marie Cosindas exhibition some years ago and some people may have thought we were pushing the pola-color process, but it was Cosindas' work that mattered. She understood the material and really used it so that she got the kind of picture that gave her satisfaction. The pola-color was particularly consonant with her needs.

"Eggleston's work was an important thing to show, a wonderful and unfamiliar kind of picture. His work should be looked at for what it is and not as a museum statement.

"I think part of the response was simply that it's difficult to write five hundred words about a man's work. It's easier to talk about museums, institutions, and curators, and not look at the pictures."

ALL THE RAJ

The photographs included in *The Last Empire: Photographs of Victorian India,* the well-received, widely reviewed exhibition at the Asia House Gallery in New York, now also a book, were often physical as well as photographic feats. The cameras used by the British photographers in India were heavy and cumbersome, the negatives hard to fix and the prints unpredictable in their quality and longevity. The hazards of Indian climate and geography were challenges, nonetheless, to the photographer-adventurers who visited the vast subcontinent some twenty years after the invention of photography.

One of the most prolific of these, certainly one of the most important, was Samuel Bourne, a partner in Messrs. Bourne and Shepherd, Simla and Calcutta, who was a producer of the stock shots of the Indian landscape, advertised by catalogue, that enjoyed great vogue in nineteenth-century England. In 1863, in *The British Journal of Photography* (to which he was to become a loquacious contributor), he gave the reader some extraordinary glimpses into the life of a commercial photographer a century ago. "From the untrodden snows of the Himalayas to the burning shores of Madras the camera is now a familiar object; and though a native from some secluded hut among the mountains where I am now situated may now and then manifest a desire to be out of its range, the majority pass it unalarmed, or their curiosity has taken the place of fear."

Bourne was one of the first to photograph the Himalayas—often requiring a string of thirty bearers to transport his chemicals, glass plates and saffron-colored dark tent—but his eye was on England. "If the photographer could only transport English scenery under these exquisite [Indian] skies, what pictures would he not produce: for I am perfectly convinced that no scenery in the world is better or so well adapted for photography on the whole, as that of Great Britain. Its mountain streams and lovely fertile valleys—its rustic cottages, overhung with thickly-foliaged trees—its cascades and waterfalls—its lakes, rivers, and verdure—are especially suited for and often so combined as to meet the peculiar requirements of the camera."

About the governmental seat of the British Viceroy, Bourne wrote: "The lover of the picturesque will find very little *material* in Calcutta. The place is totally devoid of architectural beauty, and its immediate neighbourhood of pictorial interest. Large stuccoed houses, with verandahs and flat roofs, are no doubt very cool and convenient for the Calcutta climate, but they are nevertheless very ugly; and the same remark applies to the public buildings." The Taj Mahal, however, was "this dreamlike though solid object," "'a joy for ever'."

Reflecting on his view at 14,000 feet in the Himalayas, Bourne wrote: "It was impossible to gaze on this tumultuous sea of mountains without being deeply affected with their terrible majesty and awful grandeur, without an elevation of the soul's capacities, and without a silent uplifting of the heart to Him who formed such stupendous works, whose eye alone scanned the dread depths of their sunless recesses, and whose presence only has rested on their mysterious and sublime elevations; and it must be set down to the credit of photography that it teaches the mind to see the beauty and power of such scenes as these, and renders it more susceptible of their sweet and elevating impressions." The beauty of the mountains could also be treacherous, he noted: "Take warning, photographers, and when prosecuting your toilsome art in some weary district, when the sun is hot and a smooth but rocky stream tempts your heated blood, pause before you plunge into the unknown and treacherous current."

At times, it seems, Bourne was also something of a missionary: "I observed . . . preparations were being made for the morning religious ceremony. I was not permitted to go inside, but could see a hideous wooden monster in a little dark chamber at the further end, and an old man, who, I suppose, was high priest, in the act of presenting this sublime deity with his morning repast. This consisted of some compound of 'ghee' (clarified butter), sweetmeats, and chupatties, not a particularly tempting dish for beings of less dignity than gods. This having been set before his august majesty the little door of his chamber was closed, and immediately there was set up a hideous clamour of bells and drums and tinkling of pot lids, or something very much like them, which continued for about a quarter of an hour, till the god was supposed to have partaken of sufficient of his delicious food. The priest then reopened the door, and, after bowing very low to the god, brought out the untouched food, which was forthwith carried to his own house, where I doubt not it would meet with a different fate.

"When the ceremony was over I ventured to intimate to the priest that the god had apparently not liked his food, as he had not touched it. He replied that he had eaten a little of it, but, that being a god, he did not want a great deal. I then tried to show him the absurdity of all his devotions; that the god was a senseless block which could neither eat, drink,

Samuel Bourne: *Mount Moira, South of the Gangootri Glacier,* elevation 22,621 feet, 1866.   The source of the Ganges River, the Gangootri Glacier is one of the holiest Hindu pilgrimage sites in India.

speak, nor render him any assistance; that there was but one God in the wide universe, which was so unlike his own, and so unlike the race of men, that we could not see Him; that He wanted no food, but lived for ever in the heavens, and required all men to worship Him. He listened attentively, and said that He might be a very good sort of God in His way but was inferior to his own, so I left him only more confirmed in the grossness of his own belief."

STRAND'S DOORSTEP

When in 1955 Paul and Hazel Strand bought a house in Orgeval, a small village some twenty miles from Paris, Hazel Strand began gardening for the first time. In the sprawling, trellis-covered house, she found an old book left behind by former owners—a botany textbook rather than a seed catalogue. From the book grew the reestablishment of the house's garden and from that garden a series of Paul Strand's most important photographs, a continuation of themes that preoccupied him throughout his whole career.

Then, in the last days of 1975, friends of Paul and Hazel Strand were invited to a private showing of prints for two new portfolios of Strand's work, *On My Doorstep* and *The Garden.*

Those who visited the living room of the Orgeval house, where the seventeen prints were hung, were provided a preview of one of the most singular events in the history of photography. These prints represented Strand's effort covering more than sixty years, and they also represented the achievement of an unusual collaboration. Publisher Michael Hoffman had convinced Strand after two or three years of discussion that his original prints should reach a larger public.

Until 1975, Strand had usually worked alone, or with his wife Hazel. He made no more than two or three prints from any one negative—a patient and masterly process carried out in the solitude of the darkroom. The production of portfolios therefore broached a problem with numbers that Strand had not previously encountered. On the physical level alone a sort of collaboration was called for that was the opposite of his usual method, and for a long time he had hesitated. With Hoffman, he made a selection of photographs for the portfolio and made a plan for beginning work.

The person he finally agreed should take up the challenge of working with him in the darkroom was Richard Benson, already known to American photographic circles for his care in printing the work of pioneer photographers. Discussions between Benson, the publisher and the Strands began at least a year before the project took shape in 1975, and these conversations were followed by Benson's visiting Orgeval, where he and Strand worked together for the first time to test their compatibility.

By then, another member of the team, Ann Kennedy, a young American with photographic experience, had already been part of the household for several months, cataloguing and, with Hazel Strand, responsible, for the preparatory

(continued on page 78)

JOSEF KOUDELKA

Josef Koudelka was born in Boskovice, Czechoslovakia, in 1938. For the past ten years he has traveled throughout Europe, from his native country to Rumania, to Spain and Portugal, to France, England, and Ireland, photographing primarily the nomadic and settled Gypsies.

23

LEA
The place where light shines

FOR WYNN BULLOCK
April 18, 1902–November 16, 1975

Lea is one of the things you find if you dig into the body of the word *light*, which was Wynn's meat. Wynn's mead; Wynn's meadow—now you can see how *lea* gets close to *meadow*—"and the brightness begins."

Wynn Bullock was deeply (perhaps sorely) affected by Alfred Korzybski's dictum: "the word is not the thing." Yet, there are things in the Indo-European roots of the word *bullock* that give us some light. *Bhel-*, to blow, swell; with derivatives referring to various round objects and to the notion of tumescent masculinity. It comforts this man, who makes his world out of words, to recognize that Bullock was indeed the spatio-temporal continuum he insisted he was. Not just the Old Norse *boli*, from whence BULL and BOLLIX, but such marvellous connections with the world as the BOLE of a tree; with

BOULDER; with BOWL; with BULWARK; with BOLD; even with BALEEN.

Wynn Bullock was a luminous man, with a windy, cloudy, lovely nature. I don't forget my times with him along the Big Sur Coast in the 1950's and 1960's. Very special times—it seemed that the photographers at work on those sacred places (Wild Cat Creek, Point Lobos, the Highlands, Tassajara, Carmel Valley, Monterey) whistled Sibelius's *Oceanides* as they made images.

I am one of Wynn's opposites—a poet of fact and of found objects, who is earthy, mundane, and pedestrian—and so maybe that gives me a chance to celebrate him in a way that most others would not. It allows me to be very moved by a list of plates in Wynn's forthcoming

book, *The Photograph As Symbol* (The Artichoke Press, 1976):

1.	Rock, 1973
2.	Wood, 1972
3.	Tree Trunk, 1972
4.	Wood, 1973
5.	Wood, 1971
6.	Wood, 1973

When I wrote about Wynn Bullock for *Aperture* in 1961 ("The Eyes of 3 Phantasts: Laughlin, Sommer, Bullock") I invoked the poetic Objectivists and that old spouting whale, Henry James. I'll do so again.

George Oppen is on my mind, because of a passage in Hugh Kenner's *A Homemade World* (Knopf, 1975): "The little words that I like so much," said Oppen, "like 'tree,' 'hill,' and so on, are I suppose, just as much a taxonomy as the more elaborate words." . . . It is cognate to Mallarmé's famous realization that nothing is producible of which we can say that "flower" is the name. ("I say, 'a flower,' and musically, out of oblivion, there arises that one that has eluded all bouquets.") That the word, not anything the word is tied to, is the only substantiality to be discovered in a poem gave Mallarmé ecstatic shivers; to command words' potencies was to oversee magic; to let them take the initiative was to set in motion glitterings "like a trail of fire upon precious stones." Oppen prefers to note that whatever words may be, men cannot survive without them. "They're categories, concepts, classes, things we invent for ourselves. Nevertheless, there are certain ones without which we really are unable to exist." Is the concept of humanity valid, he invites us to ask, or is it simply a "word"? "All the little nouns are the ones that I like the most, the deer, the sun, and so on. You say these perfectly little words and you're asserting that the sun is ninety-three million miles away, and that there is shade because of shadows, and more, who knows?"

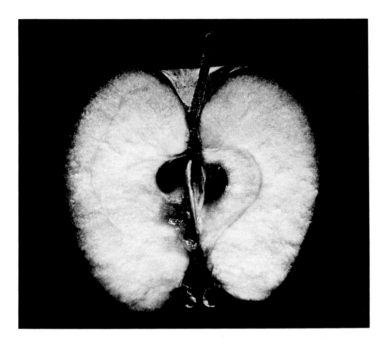

The word is the word; the thing is the thing . . . But what about that dream Charles Olson had, where Pound's shade appeared and said: "Let the song lie in the thing!" Our selves are like the famous Cloud of Unknowing, full of music and light. It's futile to try to put pins in a cloud, but here are the places—for me—where Wynn Bullock gets closest to the revealed mysteries in his prints:

"To begin with I distinguish the difference between 'seeing' and 'perceiving.' 'Seeing' is a simple almost automatic act and not to be confused with perceiving."

"For the photographer, things perceived are primary."

. . . "—a universe not only greater and more mysterious than I think it is, but greater and more mysterious than I *can* think it is . . ."

". . . too much emphasis is placed on external physical qualities of objects. An object is actually a visual *or* mental concept. It has no independent physical existence. Only events exist."

"When I feel a rock is as much a miracle as a man, then I feel in touch with the universe. Not the object rock, not form rock, but the light that is the rock."

There as the frontispiece of the book on Bullock, *Photography, A Way of Life* (Morgan & Morgan, Inc., 1973), is a reproduction of a print, "Half an Apple," 1953. In truth I relish it more than any artist's semantics. It is the veritable *Apple of the Eye*, the globular, apple-like pupil that sees what we cherish. And surely it is Wynn Bullock's insistence as a photographer that we must learn to read what our eyes show us. For him such learning is like the scales a pianist practises: the eyes, like fingers, are subtle, are limber, because they have learned how, not just how to see, but how to go on seeing. Wynn, the man, has left us, but the body of his photographic work is there for nourishment. We will make of the legacy what love permits us. Henry James was used to having the last word. It is a pleasure to give him his due: ". . . it may often remind one of the wonderful soil of California, which is nothing when left to itself and the fine weather, but becomes everything conceivable under the rainfall."

the redwood
is 'dead';

the horsetails
'live on' . . .

JONATHAN WILLIAMS
HIGHLANDS, NORTH CAROLINA

Everything in art is a symbol. The material changes but the symbol doesn't.

I have looked not for objects but for events.

I don't worry about the infinite. I worry about the finite.

The photograph does not define the tree, the tree defines the photograph.

Burk Uzzle:

The hustle comes of age

When Uzzle got married at nineteen in the small North Carolina town where he grew up, he photographed the story of the wedding dress, his mother and his bride-to-be meeting for the first time to sew the gown, and a $25 budget for the entire wedding. After the ceremony, a few dollars in pocket and the picture story in hand, they scratched off in a swirl of rice for an ambitious honeymoon in New York City. He had been reading *Popular Photography* and *U.S. Camera* for years, and attending summer short courses in photojournalism on Grandfather Mountain, and he was ready now to make his move. Yesterday it was Dunn, North Carolina, 3000 just folks, a tobacco town where *The Charlottesville Observer* and *The Nashville Tennessean* were the big time, or *The Miami Herald* and *The Louisville Courier-Journal* if you were particularly big for your britches. Tomorrow it would be the tall town itself and the big fellows from the city, home of old Coney Island infrared Weegee, riffraff sleeping on the fire escape, home of Black Star and *Life* and Magnum Photos. When the nineteen year old Uzzles zinged over the George Washington Bridge in their rented car, down and around and onto the West Side Highway, it was after midnight, which was scary enough for a couple of kids who'd been brought up to believe that the devil took over after dark, never mind all that traffic and signs that a body couldn't make sense of even with a map. They were terrified. It was enough for a while just to keep from getting run into a concrete wall by all those loose-jointed taxis with their impudent horns. They middle-laned it all the way down, the upper west side, midtown, the lower west side, and then all the way back up on the F.D.R. Drive, the lower east side, midtown, the upper east side, and then all the way back down again on the west . . . . For two hours they looped the island, down the west side and back up the east, discussing the situation every now and then like a mature married couple, until finally they couldn't face one another unless they at least tried to get off, pick an exit, one was as good as the next . . . . And so there they were, finally, in the big city, move over big city! if Dunn could just see them now! but it wasn't the Empire State Building and Fifth Avenue on a Fred Astaire Easter Sunday, it was 125th Street and Lenox, the center of Harlem on a Saturday night—oh lawdy, they would have gladly gone back to looping if they could have found the way. At last they were standing in front of the night clerk of a midtown hotel, like a couple of kids in a Dickens novel, asking please kind sir for a place to sleep. The years have taught Uzzle that no matter where you're headed you better act like you know where you're going. Even now, in his mid-thirties, for all his motorcycles and hobnobbing with the high rollers on the Avenue, Uzzle, a small frail man with horn-rimmed glasses, isn't exactly what you expect to see checking in midtown at 3:30 A.M. on a Saturday night. The clerk looked them up and down and said, you must be kidding. And they looked at one another and agreed they must be. They went back out on the street, and found their car, and got back on the highway, and got the blue blazes out of that place, getting some sleep finally in a motel in New Jersey. The next day, though, they were back in town, at the Black Star office, picture story in hand, fame and fortune calling the plays again like a sportscaster, and there they stayed, hour after hour, waiting with all the other hopefuls for someone to look at his work.

When Uzzle was twelve years old he was getting his bayonet-base SF stop-action pictures of the grade school basketball games published in the local paper. The fantasy then was a 4 x 5 Speed Graphic with a Graflex flash gun, your pockets bulging professionally with Press 40's, a backup pack of Super XX and a backup set of D cells in a work-worn vulcanite case, gray with black hardware, with your work-worn name and affiliation stenciled on top, the shutter release on the lens board mounted at a fetching angle. He manned the photo machine in the bus station in the days before it was fully automated; he worked for the local newspaper and the local studio, going from house to house on a bicycle with a Rolleicord, $1 for a glossy 8 x 10, carrying the vulcanite case in the bike basket, a perfect fit. He learned when to wait and where, and how to move when the time came; when the next fantasy shaped up, when the hustle was on.

Hour after hour, day after day, the Uzzles spent their honeymoon in the Black Star office, fewer dollars in the pocket each day, waiting amid all the cigars and ringing phones, shoulder to shoulder on the bench against the wall with all the other hopefuls in all the other offices of all the other talent brokers all over the world, virtually all of them on their quick way to stacking trays in Horn & Hardardt and then on back home to become the presidents of the local camera clubs and to reminisce the rest of their lives about New York and the Black Star office. Finally somebody looked at Uzzle's pictures, which is all it has usually taken, and in the happy end he paid for his honeymoon with pictures of his wedding. A few months later he was under contract with Black Star, and a few years later he was a *Life* staffer, and a few years after that he was proffered an invitation to join Magnum, that honey of all moons to young photojournalists who took their readings in the shadow of Cartier-Bresson. For every ten thousand photographers who want to join Magnum, one gets the chance; for every ten who get the chance, nine jump at it. Uzzle hung back for a couple of years; he was accustomed now to being the one, not the nine out of ten; in 1967 he became a member of Magnum, and still is.

The photography scene, as most of us know only too well, is chock full of intense paranoia, and its attendant isolation. There are little groups huddled together bad-mouthing one another, suspicious and compulsively defensive. Those who refuse to be pinned down in any little corner of it—like Davidson, and Friedlander, and Harbutt, and Uzzle—are especially important to us all. Uzzle is equally at home in the Witkin Gallery and on the Avenue, in *Aperture* and on the cover of *Newsweek*, as comfortable thinking and talking as most photographers are being pointedly silent. He is free, as very few

of his professional colleagues in New York are, to think that Jerry Uelsmann's work might very well turn out to be more important than all Magnum's put together, Cartier-Bresson excepted, and at the same time, as few of Uelsmann's admirers are, to believe that Philip Jones Griffiths' *Vietnam Inc.* is more valuable than all but the best of the fancy camera work and printmaking that has accompanied the exhaustion of photojournalism.

Among those he works with in New York—the photographers, the art directors, the editors, the agents—Uzzle has the reputation of a professional among professionals. One of his colleagues in Magnum, a man who has proven many times over his instinct for being in the right place at the right time, tells what it's like for a photojournalist to work elbow to elbow with him: they both appeared in Memphis when Martin Luther King was assassinated and ran on the story together for three days without sleep. When he got back and looked at his proof sheets, Uzzle was in nearly every picture he took. When the floor beneath that kind of photography began

to give way, eventually dropping *Life* magazine itself into the rubble, a lot of photographers who had grown up on the streets had to find other ways to make a living. One of Magnum's responses was to cultivate the world of annual stockholders' reports, to sell the likes of Elliott Erwitt or Bruce Davidson to RCA for $750 to $1,000 a day so that it would be possible to photograph East 100th Street whether or not anybody wanted to buy the pictures. Uzzle had never done industrial photography, and he wasn't one of the first Magnum photographers to try, but when he did it was the old honeymoon story all over again: he stood around long enough for somebody to look at his work, and a year later he was out in front, the first thing you saw when you got around the corner. If Magnum wants to sell somebody besides Uzzle to a potential new client now, they don't show Uzzle's portfolio.

There are a lot of people running around wearing different hats, but very few who can keep their head in the same place underneath them all. Uzzle can photograph motorcycle freaks one day and the board of directors of Merrill, Lynch the next not because he has a knack for moving among mutually exclusive worlds but because he sees them all as part of the same thing. Coming down off Grandfather Mountain, he might have looped the twentieth century a few times before he landed, but once he put down he knew exactly where he was and what he wanted to do with that knowledge. Uzzle has an almost Fulleresque love of technology, the sort of feel for computers and chrome and steel that we ordinarily associate with the hand crafts. Let the freaks and the directors fight if they must, he's not much interested in their argument, or anybody else's. For all his competitiveness, Uzzle isn't the least bit contentious, not now anyway, quite the opposite, in fact, gracious,

generous, unassuming in spirit as well as manner, a fine charm and sense of proportion to him; he has the moves of a man very much in command of himself and his life. Instead of writing industry off as his bread and butter, which can be a tricky kind of bookkeeping, treacherous at times, he sees in it an entree into a world that he is all the wiser for knowing, and that, from time to time, hands him personal satisfaction along with his livelihood. His Sun City pictures, some of which are in his first book, the recently published *Landscapes*, sprang full-blown out of the unlikely head of a bunch of financiers. As part of an annual report he drove around a southern California development with them, listening to them analyze the community, and returned immediately when the assignment was done to photograph the place through their eyes, a series of hard-edged acerbic pictures that cut through to the very gizzard of a world

seen as stocks and bonds. When he has to wrestle with his life, he does it, it would seem, like a Judo master. He takes the weight of what is thrown at him and uses it to his own ends; where others struggle, he dances.

If the one head is essential to what Uzzle is about, so too are the many hats; that's the way his circuit is wired, the way his juices flow. He has a Protean appetite for change, seems to thrive on it. A lot of adventurousness is predicated on stability back home, wherever or whatever home is. It may be family, place, God, previous accomplishments, usually, in the end, an unflappable confidence in one's instincts. When Uzzle turned away from his early journalism in mid-success in search of a more sophisticated image of the social landscape, those around him shook their heads and called the move a mistake. When he turned away from the social landscape in mid-success to fiddle with set-ups of styrofoam and

industrial gewgaws in a studio, he got the same reaction, even more so—imagine a Cornell Capa or a Marc Riboud looking at pictures of white on white! And now, as the large-format work begins to be taken seriously, he is back out on the streets with the Leicas, and some of the same people are telling him all over again that he is making a mistake.

For all his passion for photography as photography, the black Leicas in loving hands, miniature homemade blue denim duffle bags for carrying film, the archival prints in the clear plastic sleeves in the museum boxes, photography has never been an end in itself for Uzzle. Early on, in the days of the summer short courses in the south and the assignments as a staffer for *Life*, it was not only a livelihood but a way to go places and do things. The sexy old press pass to where the action is skipped him brilliantly across the surfaces of the world.

As he matured and came into the awareness of an inner life, he grew tired of just going to those places and doing those things, and photography became a way of articulating his spiritual life, a way to stop skipping and go deep, a ritual spread like foam on the surface where he dove.

Uzzle's career over the past ten years or so is a paradigm of much that has happened in serious photography in this country—which in turn reflects many of the important changes in the culture at large. When Robert Frost delivered a poem at Kennedy's inauguration, we were still looking to public life and to institutions for much of our nourishment, if not our salvation. Then the Bay of Pigs, and the missile crisis, and the assassination, and the war, and more assassinations, and more war, and Kent State, and Nixon. . . . As *think little* was replacing *think big* as a habit of mind, home rule undercutting the sprawling bureaucracies, as *The Whole Earth Catalogue*

was replacing the Civil Defense Manual as a check list for our survival kits, as Richard Alpert was spinning through drugs on his way to becoming Baba Ram Dass, as dumb Indians were turning out to be wiser than the think tanks, as we were beginning to listen to our bodies instead of our psychiatrists, as we were becoming more interested in art (in news that stays news, as Pound puts it) than *The New York Times,* the Uzzles moved from the city to the country, fixed up an old farmhouse not far from Woodstock, New York, and Uzzle stepped completely outside the long shadow of Cartier-Bresson, the public world of decisive moments, the small camera and the quick move, into the lights of his own new studio, private arrangements and a different pace. The anecdotes of his earlier social commentary, built around associations that were often verbal, or at least verbalizable, gave way to imagery that had little or no paraphrasable

content—which, when it worked, got well beyond an interest in the purely visual into the tilts and swings of the psyche itself. And now, as the country purges itself by cleaning out the government, Uzzle is back on the public scene, a Proteus flying by the seat of his pants, the new hand-held work showing clearly the influence of the studio. It is a much quieter, more introspective thing he does now; the associations he is making are no longer characteristically anecdotal, but visual and plastic. Perception is replacing statement; where once he was a heavy hand and a belly punch, now he floats in the vapors of things—in his words, "a journalism of the spirit."

The story of the sea god Proteus suggests an interesting way of looking at a career such as Uzzle's. Sometimes known as Poseidon's son, other times as his attendant, Proteus had the power to change forms at

will, a man one minute, a monster the next, a story close to the heart of an anxious, uncertain and insecure age. If you can stand all the quick changes, so the story goes, if you can hang in there with Proteus without demanding that he be one thing or another, he'll quiet down after a while and tell you what you want to know. It is a very rich and profound story about the illusory nature of the material world, about energy and change, about knowledge, about patience, about two radically different views of the world fused into one act . . . . Proteus is not only the nervousness of the twentieth-century materialistic west, checking the doors every few minutes to make sure the escape routes are open, the mode of reason and wit and irony and artifice, he is also at the same time the powwow doctor in his dance, the One running through its manifestations as the Many.

According to the story, Proteus has yet another power. He foretells the future. Much as Cartier-Bresson's work is haunted by the past, a European chamber music of the eye, Uzzle's is haunted by the future—and, his love affair with technology notwithstanding, *haunted* is the right word—a landscape so divorced from earth, air, water and fire as to seem almost lunar at times, a world so wired to efficiency that nothing is admitted into it that can't be controlled. Over and over again he tells us that although the superhighways and computers sing, we may become captives of mechanical dreams which are foolish at best, at worst utterly dehumanized and sterile. Uzzle is good enough, and *Landscapes* is coherent and purposefully U.S.A. enough, to call to mind *The Americans*. People are at the heart of Frank's world, their surroundings an extension of or a comment on their inner lives, whereas in Uzzle the landscape is the thing, the people, in most of his pictures, merely a function of it, like the figures that indicate the scale on a geological map. The humanist would hope that the differences are between two points of view, not a change that has occurred in the country at large in the years between the two books.

As an artist Uzzle's signature is in part his theme, in part the consummate, at times exhilarating authority of his execution. With the exception of his romantic soft-focus pictures of the hard-edged world of chrome and steel and bike-riders, and some of the large-format work, he hasn't innovated so much as refined and perfected and extended. Even when he is showing his sources—Cartier, Kertész, a touch here and there of others—what you see is how good *he* is. Or how *good* he is. Uzzle is a virtuoso, and like many virtuosos he justifies his use of others with the sheer command of his performance. And part of his signature, a large part, comes from that uncanny knack he has for boldness and delicacy in the same stroke. So characteristic, and so convincing; it sorts down to the theme of all his themes, what *really* moves him. It is probably there that he is making the artist's inevitable self-portrait, saying something again and again, perhaps, of what it is like to be a frail North Carolina bicycle boy given to bold moves in the world, wheelies amongst the music of the industrial spheres.

His signature as a man is his self-confidence. Coming off Grandfather Mountain on a bicycle, wide-eyed and bushy-tailed and moving fast, is a great approach to the wide world if you don't crack up on contact. It is a lot easier to maintain innocence and enthusiasm for life than it is to achieve it. Uzzle knows what it is like to be a winner, but he might have to learn to lose as well if he wants to take that final turn to ripeness. No matter who gets around the corner first, the dark forces are there waiting, a knowledge which is only begining to appear in his work. Still, his confidence stands strong in mid-career.

A couple of years ago Uzzle took up motorcycles, and he and his sons have been riding trail bikes lately in the meets. The bike thing isn't cut throat winner-take-all, for there is a wonderful mystique that surrounds it, a copy of *Zen and the Art of Motorcycle Maintenance* and a lot of beautiful father-and-son stuff, but the growing number of trophies in the house bear witness that the competitor in him is still kicking. The hustle gets you only part way, and he knows that. Competitiveness might be the way of some worlds, but if a work of art spins off from that spirit, it is because something finer is also there. You can court the muse, and probably have to if you want her to notice you but you damn well better not go trying to wrestle her to the floor. If you want to dance with the powers, you have to follow their lead. In Uzzle's words, "Photography used to be something you could do with your legs, but now you have to do it with your head and heart." And the true heart doesn't bend to anyone's will. About all you can do, Uzzle would say, is blow cool camera, let it happen, and see what comes out.

James Baker Hall

Signs of Life

What makes a house look like a house, a school look like a school, or a bank like a bank? What makes a gasoline station look like a good neighbor? *Signs of Life: Symbols in the American City** is intended to show that the elements of architecture have symbolic meaning and give messages about the environment that make it comprehensible and therefore usable by people in their daily lives. For example, the flashing electric sign on Route 66 tells us specifically EAT HERE and its design may suggest the kind of eating available—family dining, soft-light sophisticated, etc.—but off the main highway, suburbia's curving roads and tended lawns, its pitched-roof houses, Colonial doorways and shuttered windows, tell us without need of signs that here is a

---

*This exhibition at the Renwick Gallery endeavors to document sprawl, strip and city in relation to each other and to the nineteenth-century city. It is part of a broader effort

Even with their overall order, row houses show great variation in doorways, windows and siding. Their symbolism may be Colonial, Art Decoid or Mediterranean. *Photographs by Venturi & Rauch*

community that values tradition, pride of ownership and the rural life.

Signs of Life is an attempt to survey the pluralist aesthetic of the American city and its suburbs, and to understand what the urban environment means to people, through an analysis of its symbols, their sources and their antecedents. The focus is particularly on the twentieth-century commercial strip and suburban sprawl because in these environments the tradition of the use of symbolism in architecture has continued from the nineteenth-century city, whereas in areas more directly controlled by architects that tradition has been confused or broken by Modern architects' attempts to eradicate historical and symbolic association and decoration from architecture.

Signs of Life argues that:

—The rich pervasion of symbols and signs that existed in the historical

among social critics and architects to understand American architectural tastes and to redefine the role of the architect. *Signs of Life* indicates the need to study urban environments, especially unloved "sprawl" environmentsi and to understand the symbolic meanings people ascribe to or invest in them. The exhibition points to a radical discrepancy between the needs, tastes, and preferences of the professionals—the urban designers, architects and planners, and the decision-makers whose policies they inform—and the people whose lives they influence.

city continues in the city of today, although in different form.

    —There is a ubiquity of symbols and signs in our urban environment that we do not acknowledge.

    —The "ordinary" symbols and signs of the commercial and residential environment are significant in our daily lives.

    —In learning to understand our symbols and signs we come to understand better ourselves and our landscape; this is a necessary prelude to improving that landscape.

THE HOME

    The physical elements of housing—the roads, houses, roofs, lawns and front doors—serve practical purposes such as giving access and shelter, but they also serve as means of self-expression for urban and suburban residents.

    Winding roads, romantic roof lines, garden ornaments, colonial front doors and coach lanterns are decorative elements with symbolic overtones that residents use to communicate with others about themselves. The communication is mainly about social status, social aspirations, personal identity, individual freedom, and nostalgia for another time or place. The symbolic subject matter of residential decoration comes from history, rural life, patriotism and the estates of the rich. Suburban neighborhoods and individual houses—and particularly the decorations people add to their houses and yards once they occupy them—directly reflect these preoccupations. The housing content of TV ads, home journals, auto ads, *New Yorker* cartoons and mail-order catalogs echoes the same themes because the mass media attempt to reach their markets by using residential symbols that trigger current social and personal aspirations.

Suburban housing symbolism, however, does not tell us why people live in suburbia or much about the problems they experience in suburbia; it merely tells us some of their aspirations while they are there. Moreover, although the mass media are an interesting source of information on group attitudes to housing, they should not be taken as the last word on personal and social values in the United States. Nevertheless, the use of symbolic decoration by Americans in and around their houses is an important clue to American attitudes because it is practiced by almost all social groups, by young and old, rich and poor, renters and owners, urbanites and suburbanites.

THE STRIP

The signs and billboards we see as we drive down Route 1 or Route 66 are mostly commercial advertisements. Their words and symbols attempt to inform and persuade the potential customer in the automobile. To be seen across vast distances and at high speeds, the big sign at the side of the road must leap out at the driver, to direct him or her to the store at the rear of the parking lot. The products in the store are also advertised on the highway, on billboards sponsored by their national manufacturers. On the suburban strip, buildings are small and cheap, signs are large and expensive. The graphic sign in space has become the architecture of the highway landscape.

Most strip signs are composed of "high readers" that communicate eye-catching and evocative images, and "low readers" that give specific information, OVER A BILLION SOLD, and directions, PARK HERE. Seen from afar, the high reader suggests we slow down; then the low reader tells us why we should stop and where to go. The McDonald's arches on the strip and the wagon wheel on the suburban front lawn serve much the same purpose: each identifies its owner and refers symbolically to the owner's aspiration, commercial in one case, personal and communal in the other. However, McDonald's glowing, soaring, parabolic arches have become a national symbol. They signify the same hamburger wherever you are and suggest a familiar location for fast food for the traveler in any town. Other classic strip building types such as the gas station and the motel succeed in the same way by their familiarity and serve to identify their surroundings.

Commercial highway signs and billboards engender in the public a

Continued on page 64

The grandeur that was Rome: the spirit, if not the style, of the strip approaches that of the late Roman Forum with its eclectic accumulations. *Photograph by Deborah Marum*

Decorated house fronts are suburban billboards with flags and eagles, foundation planting, doors, porches, roofs and walls, windows, grills, shutters and ornaments as parts of the symbolic content. *Photograph by Stephen Shore*

"To own one's own home is a physical expression of individualism, of enterprise, of independence, and of freedom of spirit." (Herbert Hoover, 1932) *Photograph by Stephen Shore*

Words and symbols, rather than forms, dominate the urban space.
Photograph by John Baeder

The American bungalow is mainly a Southern and Western phenomenon. It is small, almost rural in scale, and is to the Western city what the row house is to the Eastern. *Photograph by Stephen Shore*

The rich presence of signs and symbols that existed in the historical city still persists, although in an altered form.
Photograph by Stephen Shore

The sign *is* the urban landscape. *Photograph by John Baeder*

The billboard has become the architecture of the highway and the strip. *Photograph by Stephen Shore*

On the highway, the symbol is more important than the building. *Photograph by Stephen Shore*

On Main Street, the buildings of one era are transformed by the signs of the next. *Photograph by Stephen Shore*

Each man's home is his castle. *Photograph by Stephen Shore*

range of feelings from loathing to liking. Few people want neon on their residential streets; most people appreciate the convenience of the local commerce that the signs support and of the vast parking lots and highway systems that require signs to function. If the strip is not "beautiful" in the accepted sense, it is certainly vital, an organized chaos perhaps, and probably more fun to be in than some carefully designed urban plazas that no one visits. Artists may love the strip and preservationists may loathe it, but urban planners and designers have to understand how the strip works if they are to make sensible prescriptions for suburbia.

The big sign and the little building is the rule of Route 66.
Photograph by Stephen Shore

THE STREET

WELCOME, FREE ASPIRIN, ASK US ANYTHING, STYLISH STOUTS, SURF, CITY HALL, ONE WAY, STOP.

All cities communicate messages—functional, symbolic and persuasive—to people as they move about on the street. Three message systems exist: the heraldic (signs in windows and on buildings), the physiognomic (messages given by the faces of the buildings—the columns and pediments of a Greek Revival bank) and the locational (the *corner* store, the railroad station located at the *end* of Main Street).

These systems are closely related in the city. For example, City Hall has broad stairs, a monumental entrance, a tower and flags to herald its importance and evoke associations with the past. The sign that says CITY HALL

Those glowing, soaring parabolic arches mean McDonald's and Big Macs anyplace. *Photograph by Stephen Shore*

evokes a Roman past through the style of its lettering. City Hall may be located on a public square, but it may as easily sit on a city block cheek to jowl with small-scale commercial uses. In either case, City Hall's civic importance will be suggested symbolically through the use of a "civic" architectural style and applied civic symbolic decoration.

Relations and combinations in city streets between signs and buildings, architecture and symbolism, civic pride and honky-tonk, express a messy vitality and produce an unexpected unity. It is not an obvious or easy unity but one derived from the complexity of city life "which maintains, but only just maintains, a control over the clashing elements which compose it. Chaos is very near; its nearness, but its avoidance, gives . . . force." (August Heckscher, 1962)

The Land

Albert Renger-Patzsch: Fields in snow, 1956–1958

A survey in words and images of the major exhibition of landscape photography at the Victoria and Albert Museum in London and the critics' response to it. The exhibition was selected by Bill Brandt and organized by Mark Haworth-Booth.

THE EXHIBITION: The photographers of modern times have informed us of the physical appearance of the ends of the earth, applied the unique scrutiny of the camera to places of mystery and awe, and within the last ten years have revolutionised our consciousness of the planet by showing it to us from the Gemini and Apollo spacecraft. This is the first exhibition to attempt to bring together classics from this wealth of achievement. Two hundred works were chosen by the British photographer whose contribution has been among the most brilliant in landscape photography—Bill Brandt.

Special sections of the exhibition are devoted to such masters of creative photography as Paul Strand, Edward Weston and Ansel Adams, with key works from internationally celebrated talents of the stature of Mario Giacomelli, Brett Weston, Wynn Bullock, Hiroshi Hamaya, Takeji Iwamiya, Harry Callahan, Minor White, Eliot Porter and Raymond Moore.

The rare entries into landscape photography by photographers usually identified with quite different subject matter are represented by magnificent prints from Man Ray, Brassai, Cartier-Bresson and Lartigue. Colour photography of recent years forms a large section in the exhibition. We also introduce several young photographers of outstanding promise to a larger public, and another section will reveal the striking landscape images to be found in the archives of archaeologists and geologists, the files of newspapers and the books of explorers.

—from the announcement for
The Land, 20th Century Landscape Photographs

We look at a thing and think we have seen it and yet what we see is only after what our prejudices tell us should be seen, or what our desires want to see. Very rarely are we able to free our minds of thought and emotions and just see for the simple pleasure of seeing, and so long as we fail to do this, so long will the essence of things be hidden from us.

—*Bill Brandt*

The once coherent iconography of landscape within the mind is today fragmented and shattered. The camera's lens has soared above the earth's surface in Gemini II and snapped the globe, its oceans, rivers, land, mountains, plain and desert, sparkling miraculously from afar, thrilling as though just tossed from the hand of Michaelangelo's God the Father. It has hovered closer in the air showing us clouds, fields, furrows, mounds, barrows, ranges, and peaks. It has eloquently pleaded the cause of conservation, eroded soil, dead fish floating in the polluted waters, six-lane highways tearing regardless through hill and dale, the ravaging of pit head and slag heap. It has close-focused onto the hidden beauty of pebble and seashell, pine cone and fern.

—*Dr. Roy Strong, Director, Victoria & Albert Museum*

. . . and men go forth, and admire lofty mountains and broad seas, and roaring torrents, and the ocean, and the course of stars, and forget themselves.

St. Augustine, The Confessions

In his account of the Renaissance Burckhardt describes the poet Petrarch as the first modern man to climb a mountain for pleasure. He climbed Mont Ventoux, near Avignon. Reaching the summit he looked across the panorama towards his native Bologna. He read St. Augustine's words to his brother and then would say no more.

The sense of landscape is based on displacement from the land. Continually new channels of feeling are cut back to the land in images. We live in a symbolic landscape wherever we live, language breeds metaphors and similes to keep us in that landscape. To quote a favourite saying of Bertrand Russell's, 'Love of the mountains is virtue, love of the sea is wisdom'.

—*Mark Haworth-Booth*

THE CRITICS: In the twentieth century, our vision of reality is photographic. Art ignores this at the peril of becoming irrelevant and photography bears the additional burden of justifying the artistic vision. This is a recognition of the technical nature of our reconstruction in thought of our relations with reality. The alternative is to shift the emphasis from the major purpose of the work of art to its means of achieving its aim, which is to frustrate its purpose and to reduce it to the mere exercise of style. True, art is style, but it is not style alone. In a sense, even the most stylish photographer asserts this proposition, since a photograph requires something before the lens of the camera, something, however much it may never before have been isolated and so seen, independent of the process that reveals it and yet intimately related to the technical means employed for its revelation.

There is an aesthetic that runs through the whole exhibition which probably accounts for some of the dyspeptic views taken of it. There is a frank acceptance of the idea that one might as well use the camera with all the competence at our disposal as well as use eye and directing brain. The eye might guide the lens but the lens sees what the brain conceives as independent of the eye. "One experiences this optic unconscious with the help of the camera". Benjamin has written, "just as one learns of the impulsive-unconscious through psycho-analysis. Structure, cell-tissue, with which technology and medicine strive to come to terms—all this is far more relevant to the camera than the atmospheric landscape or the soulful portrait. But at the same time the photograph opens up the physiognomical aspects of pictorial worlds existing in the minutest detail, sufficiently clear to appear in

Seen together, aerial maps of river
estuaries and road systems, feathers, fern
leaves, branching blood vessels, nerve
ganglia, electron micrographs of crystals
and the tree-like patterns of electrical
discharge-figures are connected, although
they are vastly different in place,
origin, and scale. Their similarity of
form is by no means accidental.
As patterns of energy-gathering
and energy-distribution, they are similar
graphs generated by similar processes.

—*Gyorgy Kepes,*
The New Landscape of Art & Science

it is by mixing up
intellectual and spiritual associations
with things,
and only so
that they have any importance
to our minds,

things
are nothing
but what the mind
constitutes them,
nothing

thus,
this humble habitation
becomes a shrine
of continued worship . . .

be it but
the fragment of a rock, a
decayed branch, a
simple leaf—

by an infusion:
an object of intense interest,
a relic,
priceless
as memory
itself

—*Jonathan Williams*

---

waking dreams. Now, grown large and definable, these visions demonstrate that the relationship between magic and technique is through and through a historical variable".

—*Toni del Renzio, Art and Artists*

If there is a key to their way of seeing it is the first picture in the show. What does it represent? Taken in the Antarctic in 1970 it is of a blizzard over a flat terrain of snow. From this void the world emerges by degrees. The horizon shows itself grey on white, a faint line dividing the land from the sky; and shadows appear on the earth, faint unevenness of snow. This is the beginning, a primal void of light; equally it is the empty page on which the first traces of a drawing show themselves. From these few lines a representation of the land emerges. As the journey through other pictures unfolds, the view clears to reveal intricate patterns of landscape; mountains stand in dark silhouette against the sky and the sky as a dark ground to the clouds.

In this scheme of things the world's surface is a ground for drawing; not just any drawing, but that of strong contrasts and repetitions which keep the figure on the surface. So, in many of these photographs the image integrates with the flatness of the paper. That is to say; the world is seen as a pattern or ornament before it is seen as substance and space. The search for the picture precedes the inspection of the world; or, the world is inspected as a source for pictures.

—*Ian Jeffrey*

Fay Godwin: Ridgeway: Barbury Castle clump, 1974

And this perhaps is the ultimate meaning of the wilderness and its preservation—to remind an increasingly urbanized humanity of the delicacy and vulnerability of all the living species of tree and plant, of animal and insect—with which man has to share his shrinking planet . . . if, somewhere in his community, he leaves a place for silence, he may find the wilderness a great teacher of the kind of planetary modesty man most needs if his human order is to survive.

—Barbara Ward and René Dubos,
Only One Earth

You sat on the earth as on a raft, listening to music that was not of the earth, but which ruled and arranged it. Man should be the harp articulate. When your cords were tense . . . Our thoughts and sentiments answer to the revolution of the seasons, as two cog-wheels fit into each other. . . . A year is made up of a certain series and number of sensations and thoughts which have their language in nature. Now I am ice, now I am sorrel . . . I long for wildness, a nature which I cannot put my foot through, woods where the wood thrush forever sings, where the hours are early morning ones, and there is dew on the grass, and the day is forever unproved, where I might have a fertile unknown for a soil about me . . . : All that was ripest and fairest in the wildness and the wild man is preserved and transmitted to us in the strain of the wood thrush. It is the mediator between barbarism and civilization. It is unrepentant as Greece.

—Henry David Thoreau

The real problem of the exhibition . . . I suspect, is the way it embodies the conflict between our intuitive sense of landscape and the images which obsess landscape photographers. Personal responses to landscape vary of course, but it seems possible to infer what economists would call a consistent preference—set from isolated clues: the notion of a 'beauty spot', for example; or the fact that people seem to crave high vantage points; or even the kinds of picture postcards which continue to sell in huge numbers. Taken together, they convey a sense of landscape that is couched in terms of scale, perspective, colour and the patterning of elemental masses of hills, clouds, water.

—John Naughton, New Statesman

Man has no part in the undefiled locales charted here, except in the form of the minuscule silhouettes who leave their spoor behind them like a line of neat stitching as they trail across the snow in Bradford Washburn's Climbers on East Ridge of the Doldenhorn.

Here they seem utterly subservient to the dumbfounding contours and textures of a mountainside coated with snow and caressed by vaporous cloud, mere yardsticks with which to gauge the sheer immensity of nature at its most grandiose.

Elsewhere in the exhibition, two farmers are permitted to punctuate the pared-down geometry of Gianni Berengo-Gardin's Ploughing in Tuscany, but they are no more nor less important than the other solitary inhabitants of this austere exercise in furrowed planes—a horse and a tree. . . .

But this seeming denial of a human presence is counteracted throughout the exhibition by metaphorical remind-

Our land is more valuable than your
money. It will last forever. It will not
even perish by the flames of fire.
As long as the sun shines and the waters
flow, this land will be here to give life
to men and animals. . . . You can count your
money and burn it within the nod of a
buffalo's head, but only the Great Spirit
can count the grains of sand and the
blades of grass of these plains. As a
present to you, we will give you anything
we have that you can take with you;
but the land, never.

—*Blackfeet Chieftain*

Plotinus the classical visionary
whose understanding of reality has been
integrated into both Christian and
Islamic metaphysics said: 'And if anyone
asks nature for what end she produces
(Ποιεῖ) if she consents to hear the
questioner and to speak, she will say:
"You must not question me; you must
understand, and yourself be silent, just
as I am silent and am not accustomed
to speak. What then must you understand?
That the thing produced arises out of my
contemplation (Θεχμχ), silence, and
my natural insight (theorema), and I too
am born of a similar contemplation,
and have the nature of a lover
of contemplation".' Eunead, III, 8.4.

—*Keith Critchlow*

---

ers of the body. Robert Doisneau does it with lighthearted humour in his close-up of two breast-like humps in the snow, and makes sure that nobody misses the joke by calling his picture Seins de Glace.

These, however, are only the most superficial examples of pervasive need to equate rocks with thighs, caves with wombs, sea with strands of hair, and sand dunes with the slope of a belly or hip. Sensuous, heterosexual and yet immune from any suspicion of demeaning lust, these references act as a constant reminder that photographs—for all their apparent objectivity, their testaments to the camera's mechanical skill and accuracy—are always informed by the men and women who take them.

—*Richard Cork, London Evening Standard*

Judging by . . . 'The Land', twentieth century landscape photographs, the role of the landscape painter of earlier centuries has not been replaced. These pictures, some bizarre, some masterly, some improbable and nearly all fascinating cling for their overall effect more to a specific inquisitiveness into the precise nature of the world than into an interpretation of its significance; they have more to do with geology than with art. It must be said that photography and geology are apparently excellent companions and that their relationship will undoubtedly prove to be a significant aspect of twentieth century knowledge, but it would appear, on this evidence at least, that this knowledge will be more one of information than of a heightening of visual awareness. In other words that the eye may be shown things that it might otherwise not have physically seen or recognised but it will do

Mario Giacomelli: Paesaggio Marchigiano, 1970–1975

Mario Giacomelli: Paesaggio Marchigiano, 1970–1975

Reflections from "Appalachia"
(In honor of Delius' Centenary: 1962)

dawn songs in the dews of young orange trees;
and ranging orisons; and wordless longings

sung in tranquillity's waters sliding in sun's
light;

and benisons sung in these trees . . .

in these, yes, it is the 'ah-ness', yes, it is the
course of adrenalin,
but, it is the lens opening of Frederick Delius'
luminous eye:
f/stop open—
all things measureless lucidities,

my eyes
so in tune: atonement, at-one-ment is
atonement,

what is meant by not
being able to focus two eyes . . .

they lie on the horizon,
they lie on the great St. John's River's waters
in the monocular sunlight

three miles wide
lid to lid

     —*Jonathan Williams*

Some speak of a return to Nature—
I wonder where they could have been?

     —*Frederick Sommer*

---

little to educate the eye to looking at familiar sights with a more profound understanding. These photographs are, quite simply, more conceptual than perceptual.

   —*Christopher Drake, The Tatler*

One of the most important qualities about land is its rhythm, and this is a quality which the camera seems peculiarly incapable of bringing out. Even though it may be manipulated to focus with varying degrees of clarity on different zones, it cannot simplify, to stress the underlying movement of a piece of land. Paul Nash could convey the spirit of a place, more poetically and more powerfully, in a simple watercolour than

did any of these technically superb photographs.

   —*Fenella Crichton, Studio International*

Brandt as a photographer is unquestionably an artist. So are Stieglitz and Adams, but though some are represented here who have achieved it elsewhere, no one else quite succeeds in capturing the spirit that took Sir Francis Bacon out into the rain in his open coach 'to receive the benefits of Irrigation, which he was wont to say was very wholesome because of the Nitre in the Aire and the Universall Spirit of the World'.

   —*John McEwen, Spectator*

Ansel Adams: In Golden Canyon, Death Valley National Monument, California, 1950

Bill Brandt: Barbury Castle, Marlborough Downs, Wiltshire, 1948

Bill Brandt: Skye Mountains, 1947

work, going through Strand's immense archives to find the best existing print of a negative to serve as reference for making the new prints. Thus, when work began in the dark-room, it seemed natural that Kennedy should join Benson as his assistant.

The pivot point for the project was Hazel Strand, whose attention and strength was unceasing when Strand's strength lagged—for Strand and his illness, for the visitors, for the photographs. Living and working at Orgeval permitted Benson and Kennedy an exchange with Strand that gave the prints their particular quality. At any minute of the day, and often late into the night, individual prints were submitted to Strand, technical points debated and understanding deep-ened. As Richard Benson said: "Instead of breathing sepa-rately, we breathed together."

For Benson, the print is never simply an object to be produced with mechanical fidelity to the original. Each print represents an aesthetic investigation, particularly in the case of the Strand portfolios, where negatives were made at differ-ent periods over sixty years. The distance between the prints in the archives and the artist's concept at the time they were made caused Benson to shift his own approach.

Some of the early negatives, designed to be printed on paper no longer available, had undergone various changes. As a result, Benson set out to work backwards, to eliminate as many of the intermediary stages as possible, and to arrive at the spontaneity of the original work.

The print was re-created not as a copy, but as a fresh revelation of the photograph's original presence. Sometimes a print demanded days of trial and meditation in which the slightest detail came under examination by the group. No one was satisfied until each element had found its means of expres-sion. Even after a print had been mastered, it might still undergo subtle changes of size or tonality for contextual reasons when it had been seen in relation with the other prints that made up the portfolio. Printed, toned and dried, each of the eleven hundred prints was personally checked by Strand.

The only changes made in Strand's darkroom equip-ment were those necessary to the handling of such a printing volume. Strand seemed to have worked like an alchemist, with an intuitive response to each nuance of process and chemical change. Obviously, his methods had to be reinter-preted to meet the exigencies of numbers—in this case, an edition of fifty signed examples of each portfolio. An Ameri-can developer, adequate washer, and drier were sent over to Orgeval, and for the first time a voltage stabilizer and timer were introduced. Otherwise, it was Strand's original equip-ment that served, developers were mixed for special purposes as he might have done, and a variety of papers were submitted to experiment—the diminishing quality of paper in this cen-tury being a serious obstacle to the duplication of early prints.

For the group's ambition was—in spite of the multiple edition, in spite of a necessary standardization of the process

employed—that every one of the fifty new prints of a negative should be indistinguishable from Strand's vintage print.

At the same time Paul Strand directed the activities of the darkroom from his sickbed, he worked with Catherine Duncan on the introductory texts which would preface these portfolios. Here, too, the text developed as a slow unfolding of the principles which seemed to underlie Strand's vision as an artist. Their integrity has allowed a constant interrogation of artistic purpose, a test of the acceptability of certain ac-cepted values, a research into new methods of working, cul-minating in the group achievement of the portfolios them-selves.

Commenting on this experiment, Paul Strand said that for him it had given a decisive response to the dramatic question of reproduction: "I am at war," he said, "with those who contended in the past, like Stieglitz, that only the photographer can print his own negatives. My contention is that no artist has the right to destroy the matrix of work that has become part of the social ethos. It no longer belongs entirely to him. The production of these portfolios proved there are craftsmen and super-craftsmen in the world who are so sensitive to what other people have done that they are able, through their own talents, to make a set of prints which renew with the utmost fidelity what an artist expressed many years before. With these portfolios my work becomes available to more people than was ever possible in the past. The important statement we are making, I think, is that the artist's work is there to enrich the future, and that with the understanding, love and talent of those who believe in it, who re-live it with the same engagement as the group concerned with these portfolios, then the work of art can continue to speak long after the artist himself has disappeared."

On My Doorstep and *The Garden* were published July, 1976, shortly after Strand's death at eighty-five.

Paul Strand with prints from On My Doorstep *portfolio at his home in Orgeval, France,* December, 1975.

CONTRIBUTORS

JOSEF KOUDELKA studied aeronautics at the University of Prague, receiving an engineering degree in 1961. Since 1967, he has devoted himself entirely to photography. His earlier work concerned itself largely with the theater and included a book of photographs of a production of Alfred Jarry's *Ubu Roi*. Robert Delpire, the French publisher and designer, has written: "His talent is for living with less than nothing, with the detachment and mobility of the unencumbered man without family and without a roof. With unyielding frugality and self-denial, with indifference to everything accessory, he accepts the need for discipline and goes beyond it . . . The contempt Josef has for all commentary, explanation or rationalization, and his refusal of captions and of anything didactic, is a form of questioning carried to the ultimate degree. In the incessant resurgence of questions he asks himself, Josef puts himself and the reader to the test of the reality reflected in his photographs. From this grave and stubborn quest, impassioned and unending, this book offers a fragment in the raw."

JONATHAN WILLIAMS is a poet, essayist, designer, hiker, and "ecological iconographer" of Highlands, North Carolina. He began his career at Black Mountain College in 1951 as a student of Charles Olson and, in Buckminster Fuller's words, has become: "indispensable! He is our Johnny Appleseed, we need him more than we know." For the past twenty-five years, he has published Jargon books. As well as being a contributing editor to *Aperture*, he has written "Three Phantasts: Laughlin, Sommer, Bullock" for *Aperture* 9:3, and the introduction to *Clarence John Laughlin*.

BURK UZZLE was born in Raleigh, North Carolina, in 1938 and began his career as a staff photographer on The Raleigh *News and Observer*. Since then, he has worked for the Black Star Agency, *Life* Magazine, and, finally, Magnum Photos. His book *Landscapes* was published by Magnum in 1973. He currently resides with his wife and two teenage sons in the Catskill Mountains in upstate New York.

He has written: *Photographically, my life is perhaps most interesting when dealing with these root values that are the core of my being—things and feelings and responses that are essentially American in nature. The American experience is hard to sum up, sometimes even harder to defend in view of Vietnam, etc., yet it is an experience that I find intoxicating in its excitement. The salient visual symbols of America—highways, chrome, tall buildings, zippy machines, hamburger joints, all these things turn me on; yet I feel they must be viewed not in the superficial sense as oddities. Far greater is the challenge simply to absorb them into one's being and later produce photographs which have the sense and feel of having lived with one's material long enough to have understood it deeply—and loved it.*

JAMES BAKER HALL, a writer and photographer, teaches creative writing at the University of Kentucky. Previously, he taught photography at M.I.T. and at the University of Connecticut. He is the author of a novel, *Yates Paul, His Grand Flight, His Tootings*, a book of poems, *Getting It On Up to the Brag*, and numerous stories, poems, articles, and reviews which have appeared in such magazines as *Esquire, The Saturday Evening Post, Hudson Review, Sewanee Review, Life, Poetry*, and the *Denver Quarterly*. He is a contributing editor to *Aperture* and is currently writing another novel, a book of short stories, and a profile of Minor White.

The exhibition SIGNS OF LIFE: SYMBOLS IN THE AMERICAN CITY was researched, designed, and constructed by Venturi & Rauch, architects and planners. Denise Scott Brown was the principal in charge of research and text. Steve Izenour was the principal in charge of design and production.

Smokestacks and Poplars, from the series "Rural Cathedrals"
by Minor White
Made with a Schneider Symmar F 5.6 lens
Schneider Corporation of America
154 Lodi Street
Hackensack, New Jersey   07601